DRIVING IN INDIA

DRIVING IN INDIA

RAJA UDAJI RAO PUAR OF DHAR

GYAN

Published by

GYAN

Gyan Publishing House
5, Ansari Road
Daryaganj, New Delhi-110002
Phone: 011-47034999, 9811692060
E-mail: books@gyanbooks.com

Distribution Network
gyanbooks.com
India, USA, Canada, UK, Australia

ISBN: 978-93-6433-601-7 (PB)

First Published, 1911

2nd Impression 2024

Printed at: Gyan Press, Delhi.

DRIVING IN INDIA
Author: RAJA UDAJI RAO PUAR OF DHAR

The Author.

DRIVING IN INDIA.

BY

HIS HIGHNESS

RAJA UDAJI RAO PUAR OF DHAR.

BOMBAY:

PRINTED AT THE TIMES PRESS.

1911

WITH HIS KIND PERMISSION THIS BOOK IS DEDICATED

TO

THE HON'BLE COLONEL HUGH DALY, C.S.I., C.I.E.,

LATE AGENT TO THE GOVERNOR-GENERAL IN CENTRAL INDIA,

A GREAT LOVER OF HORSE-FLESH,

AS A TOKEN OF HIGH ESTEEM AND REGARD FOR ONE BETWEEN

WHOM AND THE AUTHOR THERE HAS ALWAYS SUBSISTED

SUCH GREAT FRIENDSHIP.

PREFACE.

I do not propose in treating this noble art to offer new theories or inculcate any novel idea. The present book is an outcome of the notes made by me now and then when I was studying the subject. In the beginning I did not think that these notes would assume this form, but when they were found to be copious enough I was requested by my friends to put them together in a book form, so that they may be useful to others.

I sincerely acknowledge with thanks my obligations to Captain Hayes, Mr. James Fillis, Captain Morley Knight, Colonel De Lisle and the Duke of Beaufort, without whose assistance obtained through their respective works I would not have been able to put these pages together.

I cannot conclude without recording here the tribute of thanks I owe to Major Neil Haig of the 6th (Inniskilling) Dragoons of His Majesty's Army. Writing an introduction to a book, I may be allowed to frankly express, is entering into a partisanship with the author, and I need not say that partly to satisfy my friends and partly on account of the encouragement received from Major Haig, who has devoted the best part of his life to the study of the horse-flesh and cultivation of the art of driving, I have been tempted to have the book printed. The keen interest which Major Haig took in seeing the book written through and the careful perusal which he gave to these pages as they were in their manuscript form will leave indelible proofs of his friendship and regard for me, and I am sure his timely suggestions and assistance have much facilitated the compilation of this book.

UDAJI RAO PUAR.

DHAR, C.I., *June* 1911.

MAJOR NEIL HAIG.

CHAPTERS.

LIST OF ILLUSTRATIONS.

CONTENTS.

CHAPTER III.

DRIVING SINGLE HARNESS.

CHAPTER IV.

DRIVING FOUR-IN-HAND.

CHAPTER V.

DRIVING SIX AND EIGHT-IN-HAND.

CHAPTER VI.

TANDEM-DRIVING, UNICORN AND DEFIANCE.

CHAPTER VII.

DAKING OR POSTING IN INDIA.

CHAPTER VIII.

DRIVING THROUGH THE TOWN AND IN PROCESSIONS.

CHAPTER IX.

BREAKING TO HARNESS.

CHAPTER X.

TONGA DRIVING.

CHAPTER XI.

HINTS TO BEGINNERS.

CHAPTER XII.

HORSE AND HIS VICES.

CHAPTER XIII

BITTING.

CHAPTER XIV.

MISCELLANEOUS.

INTRODUCTION.

These following pages, written by His Highness Udaji Rao Puar, the Raja of Dhar, should prove most useful to inhabitants in India, more especially to those who have but lately arrived, and are about to set up their stable and select their stud.

His Highness' remarks about pace are most appropriate, and I would venture to point out that as far back as the days of the Old Testament bad drivers were known by their reckless pace :—

"And the driving is like the driving of Jehu, the son of Nimshi, for he driveth furiously." (2 Kings, ix, 20).

What a number of Jehus one used to see about London and on the road especially *en route* for Epsom, Derby Day, how many were delighted to be accorded the title of Jehu and how few knew or could appreciate the true meaning of that distinction.

His Highness' remarks regarding the selection of pairs for Dâk almost amount to "Hobson's choice," except that His Highness would perhaps retain his two best pairs, one for the home stage and the other as a reserve; every one I suppose has heard of "Hobson's choice," but I fancy not every one in these days knows its true meaning; so as this book is intended for novices it may not be out of place to explain here the derivation of this very common phrase.

"Tobias Hobson was the first man in England to let out hackney horses. When a man came for a horse, he was led into the stable, where there was a great choice, but he obliged him to take the horse which stood next to the stable door; so that every customer was alike well served according to his chance, from whence it came a proverb, when what ought to be your election was forced upon you, to say 'Hobson's choice.'"

The days of coaching in Europe are almost dead, the coach having been superseded by the motor; it is no longer any pleasure to drive to Epsom or Ascot races or take a day on the Brighton, St. Urbans or Hertford coach which I have many times enjoyed in olden days.

The last road coach I drove was the old Times to Brighton, about six years ago, and even as far back, as that my day's pleasure was marred by the inevitable road hog-fizzing past me and his infernal dust.

To me, though fully understanding the utility of the motor and realizing that the days of coaching in England are past, regrets abound in the knowledge that never again in the old country will the jingling of the bars and chains and the merry rattle of the hoofs and tyres on the old Macadam delight my ear, but it is not so in India, and there still remains in this country a future for coaching.

I sincerely trust that the book so simply written will be understood and appreciated by those for whom it is intended.

NEIL HAIG,

Major.

MHOW, CENTRAL INDIA,
29th March 1910.

Elephant Coach.

DRIVING IN INDIA.

CHAPTER I.

HISTORY.

DRIVING is a subject on which one can write a number of pages as it is one of the most useful arts existing in this world. The existence of this art in India can be traced so far back as the times of Mahabharata, *viz.*, 4000 B. C., when Shri Krishna drove the chariot of Arjuna. The author does not, therefore, hesitate to mention here that India did not borrow this art from the West. No doubt, one should admit that constant improvements in this art were made in the West, which were adopted in India from time to time. The art was, however, not given any impetus by way of improvement, but on the other hand it had all along been considered a "low and mean occupation" and was allowed to be left in the hands of the uneducated to remain as it was. The result was that ultimately this art was practically dying out from this country, when fortunately the timely help given to it by the West in the way of its improvement saved it from dying away.

I do not, however, propose to deal with this point at length myself, as it would waste the time of my readers unnecessarily. The art of Driving wants a lot of study in itself and one requires for it patience, courage, presence of mind, keenness, perseverance, constant practice and an observant eye. If any one were to read a number of books on the subject and not have any practice, he would never become a good coachman but on the other hand would risk his life, not knowing exactly what to do. Even the authorities hold the same views as the author does, I may quote here the following lines from an article on Driving written for the Badminton Library series by the Duke of Somerset :—

"The requisites for driving are good eyes, strong arms light hands, good nerves, good temper and plenty of practice."

Driving can be divided into two classes, *viz.*—

(1) Breaking (of horses) to harness.

(2) Ordinary driving, *i.e.*, driving well-bitted and put-together horses.

There is a vast difference between the two, for in the former one wants all the qualities described for a good coachman by the Duke of Somerset; and I may add from my own short experience that a lot of patience is also an essential qualification for a coachman. Experience shows that one who tries breaking without possessing the above qualities in himself is found quite incapable as a breaker and in many cases he spoils for ever the young horses, which can never be satisfactorily retrained or made perfect in harness. One who wishes to become a "breaker" must also be a good judge of the temper of the horses, or else he might spoil the young animals.

In the latter case, *i.e.*, driving well-bitted and put-together horses, I may say that one does not want so many qualities as in the breaking. Practice and

Dhar State Team in 1885.

patience will do him good, so far as he is concerned; because when he is only to drive "made-up" horses, which are already well-broken in harness by a good experienced coachman and regularly worked for years together, there will not be much difficulty in holding their reins and showing himself off on the box in a splendid position and style of handling his horses on different occasions on the road and getting himself called a "beauty" in driving. But this process is only meant for the aristocracy of the old or for those who aspire to be spoken as knowing everything—but not to perfection! and not for those who take a keen interest in the art and derive pleasure and *good* out of the arts they learn to the end. Thus the driving of "made-up" horses is secondary as far as driving is concerned.

The author, therefore, lays much more stress on "breaking" than on ordinary driving. A good breaker can be a driver of made-up horses at any time he desires, while *vice versa* it would take a long time.

CHAPTER II.

DRIVING—DOUBLE HARNESS.

Harness.

BEFORE putting the pair to the carriage you must see that the harness is properly put on and that the reins are correctly coupled. Unless this is done you will not be able to drive your horses with comfort to them or with satisfaction and the minimum of danger to yourself.

The length of traces and pole pieces also require the utmost attention in adjusting, but it must be kept in mind that the rein is the chief factor in harness. After thoroughly inspecting the harness and satisfying oneself, one should go round the carriage and inspect it carefully and then put the horses to the carriage. If a pair of horses is not of an equal size, the stronger and the heavier horse generally should be put on the near-side, because, in driving you always meet vehicles coming from the opposite direction and so you have to run the carriage to the near-side: thus the near-*wheel* has the hardest work to do as he has often to pull the carriage to the centre of the road.

Putting the horses to carriage.

The horse should be brought near the carriage and the outer side trace should be put first; in the meantime one of the syces* should hold the horse to the pole by

* In India one has generally two syces.

means of the pole-strap, so as to prevent him from knocking against the splinter-bar. As soon as both the traces are put the pole-strap should be fixed up to your requirements, neither too tight nor too loose for an ordinary well-broken pair. In this connection I would invite attention to the following extract from an article by the Duke of Beaufort on Driving in the Badminton Library Series, page 6 :—

" One great thing, which is much practised now-a-days and is specially to be avoided, is poling up the horses so tightly that they are like animals fixed in a vice. This is alike cruel to the horse and dangerous to the driver and his passengers. The greatest care should be taken always to leave sufficient play upon the pole pieces. By the word " play " we mean slackness when the horses are drawing with the traces and also when the animals are holding back."

After putting one horse, you put the other in the same manner ; then both the coupling reins may be fixed, after which the rein of the near-wheel should be passed on the back of the off-side wheel, and then the ends of both the reins be buckled and the driver should be ready to mount the box with the whip.

Mounting the box and taking the seat.

Before mounting the box you must have both the whip and the reins in the right hand, and then you should catch hold of the lamp iron by the left hand, at the same time putting your left foot on the *wheel-box*. * Then place your right foot on the outside roller bolt of the splinter-bar. Thus in the third motion you will be able to place your left foot on the footboard, enabl-

* (Khanjari खंजरी.)

ing you at the same time to bring your right foot thereon, when you should immediately sit down upon the driving seat. Avoid as much as you can the habit of standing up after reaching the footboard, which is very dangerous, for if the pair were to rear or move forward there is every probability of your being jerked off the box. After taking your seat you must put your both feet close together and keep the body upright and square to the front avoiding all stiffness, so that you may get well into the seat.

Position of Driver, transfer of reins.

Then pass the reins from right hand to left. In driving, never try to lean forward over the reins or to remain half-standing with unbent knees, as in the case of a horse stumbling down or shying, it is quite possible that you may unavoidably be pitched off the carriage.

Holding the reins.

There are two ways to hold the reins, *viz.*, (1) the near-rein should be placed over the fore-finger and the off-rein under the middle finger, and (2) to place the off-rein between the fore-finger and the middle finger.

Shortening the reins.

Shortening of the reins should be effected by pushing them by the right hand through behind the left. The reins should not be so tight as would prevent you from hanging them over the mouths of the animals. By constant hanging of the reins, the animals will possess hard mouths. The reins should, therefore, be so short as would allow the bits to play in their mouths; in other words you must play with their mouths by "give and take," which process could only be accomplished after a long practice.

Some of the Dhar State Carriages.

Playing with horses' mouths, position of arms and wrist.

The elbows should be as close to your body as possible, and the knuckles down to your body with a very slight bend in the wrist, so that the wrist may act like a spring.

Holding the whip.

Hold the whip in your right hand and put it across your body by placing the same on your left front ; the whip when taken in hand must be parallel to your left eye-brow, and even if it is lower, it does not matter much ; but it should in no case be allowed to go above the line of the eye-brow or at an angle of 30° to 40° from the eye-brow.

The start.

Before starting the coach, always give a word of caution, such as "Sit fast" or "All right behind;" otherwise there is a danger of the passengers being pitched off unawares, not knowing that the coach is going to start. In starting the horses there is generally a tendency of flicking a whip or calling "pull up," "hold up," and sometimes many people give a whistle, which to my mind is quite unnecessary and for which I may quote an authority (*vide* article by the Duke of Somerset, in the book "Driving" of the Badminton Library Series, page 193) :—

"Teach your horses to standstill after you are on the box, till you wish them to move, having all reins properly in hand, raise it gently and they will start at once; you should never have recourse to that horrible new custom of crying up "Hold up" * in a stentorian

* Or more commonly "Pull up," which is ridiculous.

voice which is most unseemly and quite unnecessary, or clicking with your tongue—a regular cabman's trick, both only intended for Bath waggon-horses in the olden time."

In starting shorten the reins and just feel the horses' mouths lightly, thus giving them the "office" to start and at the same time, if necessary, give them the word to go. I have found among few of the native coachmen that when the syce is standing before the horses and when they (the coachmen) want to start them, they will say "*Chhor do*," *i. e.*, "Let them go," equivalent to "Stand away." Thus knowing from the daily practice that by this sign they have to start, the animals move on at once. I had a couple of pairs, *viz.*, *Bays and Browns, as also a team of Bays*, who were quite accustomed to the above practice, so much so that all of them would stand still in the carriage, even if there be no one before them or on the box; on the other hand, when there was nobody in front of them but the coachman on the box and if he were to say "*Chhor do*" they would start, otherwise they would stand still. These are, however, particular instances, but the general rule which I give below may safely be followed :—

"Holding all your reins properly in hand, raise them gently and they will start at once."

Starting the horses gently.

I wish to force the point of always starting the horses gently for the following reasons :—

If you use your whip at the moment of starting—as soon as you take your seat on the box, the horses may after a short time get into the habit of not coming to the carriage to be put in, thinking they would be hit as soon as they were coupled up : thus when they come to the carriage and are put in, they will frequently try to start as soon as possible; they will not even give you time to mount the box, which is rather dangerous and will get into the vice of "plunging forward," which habit may be developed to such an extent that either they will begin to rear or jib if not allowed to "plunge forward," which means the ruin of the character of the animals. Therefore, to avoid all these vices and risks, I think you must start your horses "gently."

The Pace—Taking corners gently.

After going at walk, say for about 20 to 30 yards, put the animals into trot. Never try to put your horses into centre except on very special and rare occasions, and gallop them only in unavoidable circumstances. The usual pace should be between 8 and 9 miles an hour ; corners should be taken as gently as possible. It depends much on the pace you go and the angle at which you take your corner. This can better be learnt by experience rather than from books ; but I would prefer to go always gently at the corners as much as practicable.

The use of Brake.

One should use his brake as seldom as possible, save in cases of emergency and unavoidable circumstances, for the following reasons explained by the Duke of Beaufort in his article,* which speak for themselves :—

"In another part of this work we shall touch upon the question of the application of the brake for stopping the

* Badminton Library Series on "Driving," pp. 6-7.

carriage; but we must here particularly impress upon the young (and in not a few cases the hint may be judiciously and usefully extended to the old) coachmen that, as a general rule, a great deal too much use is made of the brake. It is a great relief to a horse when he makes a slight dissent to come out of his collar, so that the carriage travels along behind him without any exertion on his part. Almost invariably, however, the spectator will observe that the moment the carriage goes down ever so slight a declivity, the coachman claps on his brake; and the consequence is that the horse is always pulling, the practical effect of which, so far as he is concerned, is that he always seems to be going up-hill. It should be the object of the driver to make the horse's work as easy as possible and to relieve him from this unnecessary strain. If the descent be severe the brake should of course be applied; but coachman must discriminate, and there can be no doubt that most of them are far too apt to employ this comparatively modern contrivance."

I may give here an instance of my own personal experience as to how a would-be serious accident was avoided by applying the brake in proper time. In January 1908, while going to the house of my father-in-law with a party of about 10 gentlemen in my Brake, to which I had only the wheelers and the pace at which we were going was about 8 miles an hour, I noticed before coming to a corner, a peculiar sound from the near fore-wheel; but as I could not distinguish positively from which it was, soon after, just as I was taking a corner the tyre of the nearside fore-wheel went clean off and the body began to drop down. Immediately I put the whip in my left hand thumb, the right leg across the reins and applied the brake and thus managed to pull up dead within a couple of yards

The use of the coupling-reins.

The adjustment of the coupling-reins depends upon the circumstances, requirements and the experience of the coachman. No hard and fast rule can be laid down in this respect.

Driving with one hand (left).

Driving with one hand (left hand) is very essential, because you have more control on the animals than with both the hands. In shortening the reins you have no trouble if you are driving with one hand, because you just place your right hand in front of the left and push those required to be shortened through the left hand.

Going round a corner.

In going round corners the rein of the required direction should be shortened. By driving with one hand you can easily use your whip (right hand) to any of the animals you wish at the right moment, and specially at the time of taking a corner, if the inward horse was to try to cut it sharp, you can keep him out by shortening the opposite rein, or if necessary by hitting him with the whip which will prevent him from cutting the corner sharp. On the other hand if you drive with both the hands, *i.e.*, by holding the reins in both the hands, it looks very awkward and at the time of stopping you have to bring your both the hands right up to your ears. I have seen in many cases that one cannot have an effectual stop as he can have by driving with one hand. A man in the habit of driving with two hands frequently requires a third.

When both of your hands are engaged in holding the reins, you cannot hold your whip well nor can you use it properly at a moment when you wish to make use of it. By holding the reins in both the hands and then trying to hit the animal, the off-rein would get slackened and the horses then would dash to the left.

Never use whip when right hand is on reins.

On the other hand, if you drive with one (left hand) and wish to give a smart flick to the horse, you can do that easily without touching the reins which would keep the animals on their path, and at the same time you would be able to use your right arm as a help to the left.

Therefore, many years' practice shows that the mode of driving with one hand (the left) is the best. I may quote here an extract from the Duke of Beaufort's article* on the subject :—

"In former times, when there was no break for carriages, it was absolutely necessary for a man to drive with one hand, because when going down a steep hill with a heavy load, and with tired and jaded horses, it was very often only possible to keep in the road by the use of the whip. Horses have a habit of hanging, so to speak, to one side or the other, to such an extent that nothing but a smart flick over the shoulder or the neck will straighten them, or prevent the vehicle from running into the ditch ; and if, before the days of breaks, a coachman had attempted the wretched modern practice of driving with a rein in each hand, he would most assuredly have upset his load."

Turning round carriage at a stand-still.

When your carriage is standing in such a position that there is just room enough for you to turn it round

---

* *Vide* Badminton Library Series, "Driving," page 7.

without moving a yard forward, you should take it a few paces on one side and then put your right arm about 6 inches in front of the left hand, if you are turning to the right, on the off-side rein and draw your arm gently to your body, and at the same time you must shorten the nearside rein by sliding the left hand up to the right, which will prevent the near wheeler from coming round more quickly. The same course should be followed for turning round to the left. This process cannot be done with an unbroken pair, jibbers, kickers, etc. You must have well-broken and quiet horses and a carriage of full-lock. The only reason of giving this method of turning round a carriage at a stand-still is that in India one always has to take a turn round in a narrow lane or street, where he has no alternative but to turn his carriage at a stand-still.

Pulling up the horses.

In pulling up your horses it mostly depends upon the pace you are going. If you are going at an ordinary pace—say about 8 to 9 miles an hour, you should not pull your horses dead, the reason being that, if you stop them dead, the carriage will run on their hind-quarters which may cause them to bolt or kick, likewise, they may sprain their shoulders or hocks or may get bruises and cuts to their hind-quarters. So, to avoid all these risks, you must decrease the pace—say, at 20 to 30 yards from the point you are going to stop. In that way you will be able to stop your horses without running any risk or danger, etc.

Taking horses out of the carriage.

When you have stopped the horses, the syce or the syces, as the case may be, jump down or run to horses' heads. Then unbuckle the reins and throw them on the back of each horse; in the meantime the syce has to take out the coupling rein and loosen the pole-strap; after this take the inner and outer traces respectively of the horse and put them across his back; similarly you do with the other horse too. Then unpole the horses and lead them forward with care that neither their hind-quarters nor any other part of their body touch the pole or any part of the carriage, because if they are touched there is always the danger of either their kicking or getting excited and running away from the carriage, in which case there may ultimately devolve the difficulty of putting them to the carriage. You must always take out the horses of the carriage quietly and calmly. The more quietly you take them out the better and safer it is.

Driving up-hill.

When you are driving up a hill, always work your horses together and keep them up to their collars. It is not advisable to allow one of them to hang on because the other horse will have to do the whole work; and if the hill is a steep one he may get tired and stop, which would endanger the driver in making another start and finishing up the hill. This is a general rule for an ordinary broken pair; but when you get in a pair—a willing or free-going horse with a sluggish companion, then it is rather difficult to make them work together. Under the circumstances the best way is to keep the sluggish animal up to his collar cantering, if necessary, by touching him with the whip on the shoulder, also by playing with his mouth, both of which should enable the coachman to keep his traces tight and thus make him work level with the free-goer. In this way the work will be distributed equally. Do not make your pair canter in going up a hill, because there is nothing worse than to tire them out and spoil their chests as the whole weight of the carriage in going up a hill falls on their chests and shoulders, which may ultimately sprain the pectoral muscles and the shoulders.

I have seen horses dropping dead in a harness immediately after reaching the top of a hill, simply because their coachman had galloped them or kept them cantering through the whole time during the ascent. It does not matter much, if you in going up a slight hill gallop your pair, because it helps them to pull the carriage at ease. Never mind if your horses walk up a hill, it is better than to make them canter, because in walking up a long hill the horses have not to exert themselves as much as they had to if they had cantered, and throughout they will have a steady pull.

Going down-hill.

You must be careful, in going down-hill, to see that the horses do not "hang," so to speak, on one side or the other. Experience has shown that horses should be driven as slowly as possible, and be kept straight. In a great descent, the syces should be made to walk on both the sides along with their horses to be ready in case the carriage goes to one side of the road. The syces of either side can help the coachman by putting their hands on the body of the horse between the collar and the pad, so that the horse may know by feeling the sensation of the hand of the syce, touched between the collar and the pad, that he is not to hang, thus enabling him to go straight. Suppose you have only one syce, then you should make him go along the side of that horse which you are not sure of keeping straight during the descent. In India there is always a narrow space found with a lot of dust at the edge of the road. So you should put the two wheels on either side of the road on that edge which will enable the carriage not to slip down much.

Use of whip in going down-hill.

You should remember to shorten the reins according to your requirements in going down-hill ; also do not forget to hold your whip in the hand, for if the horses were to hang on one side or another nothing would straighten them, as well as a smart flick on the shoulder or neck.

I may just record my experience here. I was once driving a pair out of my Palace-square at my capital, through the main gate called "Delhi Gate," the way out of which is a sort of a descent about 26 yards in length, where it slopes away into the outer square of the Palace. The width of the road is 19 feet, and there is a brick-work railing on both the sides, gradually sloping from about a couple of feet to 9 inches. The level of the top of this slope at the Delhi Gate is 10 feet higher than that of the latter square, and it sinks with a bit sharper gradient. My carriage had run down only a couple of yards near the top of the slope when the near-side horse in his hanging gave a push to the off-side one, who got clean off the brick-work railing about 4 feet below the side of the road, down which I was driving. Luckily I gave a smart flick of my whip in time to the off-side horse, as it was too late to flick the near-side one who being very strong jumped up again on the road. The cause of what would have been a nasty accident lay in the neglect in not taking the whip in hand at the time of commencing the descent.

CHAPTER III.

DRIVING SINGLE HARNESS.

THE driving of single-harness is practically worked on the same principles as those of double-harness. So also is the method of holding the reins, and I would therefore ask my readers to refer to Chapter II, page 6, for further particulars.

Taking corners gently.

In driving single-harness care must be taken to see that the corners are not taken sharp, as the cart being of two wheels, there is every possibility of its getting capsized immediately when knocked against a lamp post or a stone.

The pace.

The pace should not be jerky, as it would strain the shafts and also make the passengers feel uncomfortable.

Selection of horse.

The selection of the horse should be according to the size of the vehicle.

Breaking the horse.

It is always better to break a young horse first in the double-harness on both the sides of the pole before putting him into the shafts.

A jibber.

If a horse were to jib in single-harness, there is nothing but to back him up and make the syce put a rope round one of his fore-legs and drag him for a few paces; when once the jibber starts the syce should at once drop the rope and get aside, so that it may not be entangled in the legs of the horses.

CHAPTER IV.

DRIVING FOUR-IN-HAND.

IN this Chapter, I will only confine myself to the method of holding four reins. As for the position of the driver and the general method of holding the reins, I would ask my readers to see Chapter II, page 6, in which the subject has been fully dealt with.

No one should ever attempt to drive four horses until he has learnt the art of driving a pair *properly*. I mean he should not only be able to drive made-up and well-bitten pairs but all kinds and sorts of pairs, a pair of sluggish horses or a free goer with a lazy one or both free horses and horses of different kinds of vices. Secondly, it is also very essential that one should have learnt the use of altering the coupling reins, so as to enable him to distribute the work equally between the free horse and a sluggish one.

Selection of a team.

It solely depends on the choice of the person who drives a team as to whether to have the leaders and wheelers of equal size or the leaders bigger than the wheelers. But generally it is preferred to have the wheelers and leaders of equal size or the wheelers little heavier than the leaders. The same rule would apply to Tandem, Unicorn, Six-in-hand, Eight-in-hand and Defiance.

Putting the horses to the carriage.

In putting the team together, the wheelers should be put first and then the leaders, and care should always be taken not to knock hind legs of the wheelers or the leaders against the splinter-bar or bars. It depends upon the choice of the coachman whether to put pole-pieces to the leaders or cross their inward traces so as to keep them together in case one of them were to hang out. This we will deal with later on.

It is very essential that the pole-strap of the wheelers should always be very strong and in serviceable condition as much extra strain falls on it. Therefore, our first attention should be centred, before putting a team to this particular part of the harness, to see whether it is in a serviceable condition or otherwise. After putting the leaders in, the leaders' reins should be placed through the terret on the outside of the bridle of the wheelers through the centre terret of the pad. Thus the team will be ready to start. Now-a-days this method of running the leaders' reins through the terrets on the outside of the bridle has generally been adopted and preferred to that of running the leaders' reins over the wheelers' heads.

It is always safe not to drive a team in snaffles and not to buckle the ends of the leading reins.

The reins.

After taking and passing the reins from the right hand to the left, the general method of holding the reins is to place the near leader's rein over the left fore-finger, the off-leader's between the fore-finger and the middle-finger, the near wheeler's between the same and under the off-leader's and the off-wheeler's between the middle

The Author driving a Four-in-Hand.

and the third finger. In holding the reins the thumb and the fore-finger should not be used but only the three lower fingers, in order to have a firm grip, the thumb and fore-finger being used only when looping.

The start.

Thus adjusting the reins we should gently feel the mouth of every horse or give a click of the tongue, if necessary, to indicate them to start. In starting we should invariably make the wheelers start the coach and not the leaders, as the latter's starting may create unpleasantness or excitement with the wheelers who when dragged by the leaders may begin to play a fool ; to effect this we should touch them between the pad and the collar with the whip if they require an indication. When the coach has fairly been started off, then we might make the leaders work their share.

Leaders to work up-hill.

The leaders as a rule should not be made to do much work when going on a flat or level road or a long journey, but they should only be called upon to give extra assistance in going up a hill.

Shortening the reins.

The shortening of the reins can be effected by putting the right hand in front of the left and pushing those required to be shortened through the left hand. But the novice will find it easier to shorten the reins from behind by pulling them through the left hand. This is a habit which should be stopped in its infancy.

Turning Corner.

In going round a corner, the pace should be reduced and the leaders' bars slackened, otherwise the wheelers will inevitably be dragged to cut the corner sharp. As regards turning to the left or to the right, I cannot recommend a better and shorter method than Captain C. Morley Knight's given on page 88, para. 2, of the book "Hints on Driving." He writes :—

"To the left.—With the right hand seize the near-lead and wheel reins under the lower fingers ; then either pull those reins up towards the centre of the body, which will shorten them, or allow the left hand to go slightly to the front, which will slack off the right reins, or better still, combine both these motions, the result being the same in each case, that the team will go to the left."

"To the right.—Take hold of the off-lead and wheel reins with the lower fingers of the right hand, and treat them in the same way as described for the left reins, when the team will go to the right.

The latter of the two methods is by far the best and the one most usually employed, the other only being possible with very perfectly broken teams, as obviously only very little pressure can be put on."

Inclining.

In taking a gentle turn it is not necessary that the bars of the leaders should be slackened, it being sufficient to pull the lead rein with the right hand retaining a slight coil on it, at the same time holding the wheel-rein of the same side. This method is also applicable while taking an incline on the road.

There is also another way of making the team incline to the left or right as the case may be ; in the former one has to turn his left hand knuckles upwards and bring them across the body from left to right which

Major Neil Haig with his Regimental Team.

will make the horses incline to the left, as thereby the reins of that side will be shortened, while in the latter case one has to bring his left hand down to the left with the knuckle of the fore-finger downward, and that of the little-finger uppermost which will incline the team to the right.

Going down-hill.

The leaders should be allowed only to carry the bars by slackening the traces, care being taken that the traces are not so much slackened as to allow the whole weight of the bars on the pole, thereby putting extra strain on the wheelers' necks. To enable this the driver will have to take a "loop" which can be effected in two ways (1) by pulling the lead reins back about 2 to 4 inches, placing them o the top-finger of the left hand and pressing them down with the thumb, and (2) by pulling and placing the leading reins in the right hand, which should be kept close together with the left hand wrist. Thus in the former case, when the descent ends, the driver will have the leaders ready to do their share of work by only a lift of the thumb, while in the latter he will only have to take his right hand off the leading reins. This method should be used and will be frequently required to be put into practice when crossing small culverts which are numerous on the roads in India.

Use of whip.

Howsoever perfect a team may be, still at times the use of whip is quite indispensable, on the proper application of which the safety of the coach may well depend; and, therefore, it is very essential for one who desires to drive a team to be able to play with his whip properly.

But this art cannot be achieved without much practice, so I may quote a simple method here:—

"A very good way to learn to catch the thong neatly round the stick is this:—Chalk a large pot-hook or S on the wall; stand opposite to this with the whip held in the proper position, the thong undone and the point of the lash under the middle finger of the right hand, the fore-finger rather pointed up the stick; then with the point of the whip quickly follow the line as traced on the wall, beginning from the bottom end, and moving it across from left to right. The top part of the S should be done by a back turn of the wrist, first upwards and then downwards, which will bring the fingers uppermost at the finish. Never let the point of the whip drop at the beginning of the S and never hit at the thong, but on the contrary make it come up to the stick. If you find that the thong is caught rather too low down, it can very easily be sent up higher by catching it again as above, but with rather a shorter and more jerky motion, in fact describing a small S."

"This is done almost entirely by the wrist, with only a slight movement of the arm."

"Having caught the thong, the next thing to be done is to take out the loop which will be found in the middle of the stick, so that all the turns should be from right to left; otherwise it will very soon become undone. To do this, lower the stick so as to enable the left thumb to seize the loop (taking care not to move the left hand from its correct position while doing so); now move the whip and out to the right front as far as possible, keeping the wrist well bent and holding the lash tight with the left thumb. This movement will take off the

The Author in the Mhow Horse Show.

turns on the lower end of the stick, now place the whip under the left thumb, and turn the spare end of the lash once or twice round the handle. With the right hand retain the point of the lash securely under the inside of the right thumb, which will prevent the thong getting loose. If the point slips up, it can be pulled tight again by catching hold of it with the left thumb and fore-finger, and drawing the right hand away."

"The thong should be kept pliable by being rubbed with salad oil or mutton fat: otherwise it will be found difficult to keep it in its proper place when caught." (*Vide* Captain C. Morley Knight's "Hints on Driving," pages 106-109.)

Bringing the thong back after hitting the leader.

It is also important after hitting the leader to be able to catch back the thong without hitting the wheeler or the gentleman on the "box." To do this it is necessary to send the thong out to the front over the leaders with a circular motion and to hold the stick vertically, which will bring the thong into the hand of itself.

Straightening the team.

When the team is not going straight, *i.e.*, leaders going to the left and the wheelers to the right, one has to straighten them by shortening the centre reins, *i.e.*, the off-lead and the near-wheel reins by catching them with the right hand and placing in front of the left hand and then sliding the left hand upto the right or pulling them through from behind the left hand. In case when the leaders are going to the right and the wheelers to the left, the near-lead and the off-wheel reins should be shortened in the manner stated above.

Pulling up.

Before pulling up slacken the pace of the horses, shorten all the four reins by bringing the left hand up to the right or pulling all the reins through from behind as stated above, and then draw both hands towards the body which will enable the team to come to a stand-still. If the team were to gain the better of the driver, he could have extra assistance by placing his right leg over all the four reins which will enable him to pull them up with ease.

Taking the team out of the coach.

There are two ways to take out the team. The one which is general is to throw the reins down with both hands outside the wheelers, the other being to take out the leaders first and then the wheelers.

DHAR TEAM IN THE SHOW.

CHAPTER V.

DRIVING SIX AND EIGHT-IN-HAND.

General.

ABOUT driving 6 or 8 horses, it is always said that the coachman has no control over his leaders, but I must say that it is an unfair remark, because this form of driving is not meant for mere novices but for those alone who have iron-nerves, perfect hands and know the "aids"—the art of driving thoroughly, whip, rein and voice and have experience at the back. As I have already discussed the "aids" in different chapters and heads separately, I do not think it advisable to recapitulate them here, but suffice it to say that one, who has thoroughly learnt the proper use of the "aids," has not only the command but the capability of conveying his orders to any of his horses direct and carrying them out with precision. For a driver of this calibre, it is just the same whether he drives a horse, a pair or four, six or eight-in-hand, but to make a special study of any of these he must have both patience and experience.

For driving six and eight-in-hand we must have thoroughly broken and well-bitted pairs and the principles of driving four-in-hand apply to this also.

Putting together Six-in-hand.

The wheelers should be put first, next the "No. 2 lead" and then the "No. 1 lead." It is very necessary that the pole-piece should be fixed to the "No. 1 lead" and their inward traces not "crossed," as they are done for the leaders in a team of four-horses, because the traces of the "No. 1 lead" are not fixed to the splinter bars, but they are hooked as is done in tandem without bars.

In India drivers of six-in-hand and eight-in-hand use both the hands while driving, but instead of that, if the above method is adopted, the driver will have better control over his team than when driving with both the hands.

Holding the reins of Six-in-hand.

The way of holding the reins of 6 horses is the same as that of four-in-hand, the only difference being in their adjustment between fingers. We may call (for the sake of our convenience) the foremost leaders (or the third pair) as the "No. 1 lead" and the second as "No. 2 lead."

In holding the reins one is to have the near "No. 1 lead" over the left four-finger, the off "No. 1 lead" between the fore-finger and the middle finger, the near "No. 2 lead" between the same and under the off "No. 1 lead;" the off "No. 2 lead" between the middle and the third finger, the near-wheel between the same and under the off "No. 2 lead" and the off-wheel between the third and the little finger.

The process of running the reins of the "No. 1 lead" is the same as that of the leaders in a team of four.

The start.

Invariably the wheelers should start the coach and not the "leaders;" when the coach has once been fairly started the leaders may be worked to do their share.

Taking and going round corners.

When going round a corner the pace should always be checked and the traces of the "leaders" slackened the leaders being well taken out with the wheelers so as to avoid cutting the corner sharp.

Frequent use of the right hand.

The frequent use of the right hand will be necessary while going round a corner by taking a "loop" with the right hand and also at the time of taking draught of the "leaders" in going down-hill, placing it close to the left hand wrist as it will not be manageable to hold the "loop" under the left hand thumb, till the descent as well as the corner ends.

Pulling up.

Before pulling up all the reins should be shortened as explained in Chapter II, at page 6, and then catching the leading reins with the right hand, both the hands should be pulled back towards the body.

Taking the teams out of the coach.

The front two leading teams should be taken out one after another, after which the wheelers.

Method of holding the reins of eight-in-hand.

The way to hold the reins of eight-in-hand is to have the near-leader's of "No. 1 lead" over the left fore-finger, the off-leader's of "No. 1 lead" between the fore-finger and the middle finger; between the same and under the off-leader's of "No. 1 lead," the near-leader's and off-leader's of "No. 2 lead;" the near-leader's of "No. 3 lead" between the third finger and middle finger; between the same and under the near-leader's of No. 3, off-leader's of No. 3 and near-wheeler's; and between the third finger and little finger the off-wheel rein.

CHAPTER VI.

Tandem-driving, Unicorn and Defiance.

Tandem-driving.

IT is driven more or less on the same principle as that of four horses; so the readers will refer to Chapter IV on "Driving Four-in-hand."

In driving a tandem you must have a well-bitted and well-put-together team in order that there may be very few chances for any mishap.

A team of ponies would look much smarter than the horses for the tandem.

While driving the tandem it is very necessary to see that the pace of the leader is checked and the traces slackened before going round a corner. If on the contrary the traces of the leader are not slackened, the wheeler will inevitably be dragged by the leader and knocked against a wall or post as may be the case and the trap turned over.

Care should be taken that the traces of the leader are not too long; otherwise when slackened in going round a corner there is every possibility of the leader getting one of his hind-legs over the trace, thus creating some unpleasantness to the driver for the time. If the leader gets into the habit of turning round, which, as a rule, is due to the sheer bad handling of the reins on the part of the driver, he should be corrected by means of the application of whip, at the moment he turns round.

While driving the tandem one has to make use of his right hand frequently with quickness on the reins so as to keep the team going straight.

Unicorn.

Unicorn means driving one horse in the lead and two in the wheels. The mode of holding the reins of the unicorn and the general way of driving it are the same as those of four horses. The leading reins should be placed through the terret on the inside of the bridle of the wheelers through the centre terrets of the pad and not on the outside, there being only one horse in the lead which is to go in the centre, and not on the sides as in the leaders in four-in-hand. The driver should only remember while going round corners that he has got only one leader and not two. This comprises all the difficulties both of a team and a tandem and the horse more than ever. A quick right hand and whip are important adjuncts.

Defiance.

Defiance means driving three horses abreast in the lead and two in the wheels. In driving a defiance two extra pairs of reins are required for the centre horse to be attached to the coupling reins of the leaders.

As regards holding the reins and the principles of driving, the details given in driving four-in-hand are applicable to the defiance also.

CHAPTER VII.

DAKING OR POSTING IN INDIA.

Daks essential in olden days.

BEFORE the motors took the place of the horses for Daking (posting) there had always been a custom and necessity of using horses from the nearest railway station to the place of destination, *viz.*, the Capital of a Native State. I think I am right in making a remark here that there are still some Native States left far in the interior without railway communication, as much as from 30 to 40 miles from the nearest station, and none felt the difficulty more in olden days than these States in arranging for the conveyances by laying Daks for guests, Sirdars or officials, or sometimes for the Chief himself. The Capital of my State being peculiarly situated at a distance of 33 miles from the nearest railway station, I had special opportunities to go into the details of the subject, and the hints which follow as the result of my past experience are given with a view that they may be useful to those States who have not yet adopted the modern means of travelling,—I mean motors. As my late lamented father, Maharaja Sir Anand Rao Puar, K.C.S.I., C.I.E., had many European friends in Mhow and many other parts of the Indian Peninsula, from where they used to come to visit him, and also to see the antiquities of Mandoo, which is 24 miles from Dhar, the Capital of the State, it was very essential to have the Dak laid constantly from Mhow to

Dhar (33 miles) and sometimes to Mandoo (24 miles) from Dhar. Generally in this part of the country, we post horses on Daks at an average distance of 8 miles from each stage, the chief reason being that the stifling heat of the country is very trying on the animals, and takes much out of them and ultimately makes them unfit for work, and secondly the animals are driven by a majority of indifferent coachmen, who do not take care of the animals while driving or after taking them out of the carriage but simply know to drive their pairs at tremendous speed so as to reach their destination earlier than usual, in order to get *Inam* (reward) from the gentlemen whom they have driven ; so naturally one can guess if horses on Dak are driven simply for the sake of "*Inam*" how much would be left of them within a week after taking so much work out of them. Then they are left to the mercy of their respective syces on the stages, who in many cases steal gram and starve the animals ; no wonder if the animals drop dead in harness on account of starvation and fatigue.

Reliable Syces on Dak.

There must, therefore, always be a rule to send reliable syces on Daks, or at least one with a pair, giving him some travelling allowance (batta) for the days he is out, which keeps him far from the temptation of robbing the animals of their feed. The distance for each pair on Dak should be on an average from 8 to 9 miles.

Points of importance in laying a Dak.

In laying a Dak the following points have to be considered :—

(1) Number of pairs in the stable.

(2) Which of them are fit to go out.

(3) How many of them can be spared from ordinary routine work of the State.
(4) Number of miles to be travelled.
(5) Gradient of the road.
(6) Abilities of the coachman driving the pairs.
(7) Which carriage should go on Dâk.
(8) Weather.
(9) Harness.
(10) Pace.

The above points should be considered in the following manner :—

(1) *Number of pairs in the stable.*—Spare as many pairs as you can, *i.e.*, if there is a Dâk required for 30 miles, you must lay 4 pairs or at least 3 pairs if you are short, but not less than that, so that too much strain may not fall on the horses.

(2) *Which of them are fit to go out.*—Those horses which are acclimatized and which are strong enough to bear the heat and work should be sent.

(3) *How many can be spared.*—It depends upon the circumstances of the routine work as to how many pairs out of the lot can easily be sent on Dak.

(4) *Number of miles to be travelled.*—This should generally be divided by 8, so that one can know generally how many miles a pair will have to cover.

(5) *The gradient of the road.*—The strongest and most reliable pair should be put on a steep and long gradient and also on a long stage.

(6) *Abilities of the coachman.*—The coachman who knows his work of driving thoroughly, who does not drive his pair fast except under unavoidable circumstan-

ces, who is well experienced and who takes a great deal of care of his animals while driving, should be nominated for Dâk purposes.

(7) *Which carriage should go on Dak.*—The lighter the carriage the easier it is for the horses to drag on long distance and also for increasing the pace. Generally I used to send out a victoria, or a wagonnette or a light landau.

(8) *Weather.*—It should be judged, *i.e.*, in the monsoon the carriage should travel slowly than in an ordinary fine weather, so that the horses will not get sore-shoulders on account of heavy roads.

(9) *The harness.*—The following harness should be used for Dak:—

1 pair of collars with leather pads or false collars.
1 pair of blinkers with bits and curb chain.
2 pairs of traces.
1 pair of reins.

(10) *Pace.*—The average pace during monsoon and on bad roads should be from 7 to 8 miles an hour only, and in fair weather and good parts of the road the speed may be from 8 to 9 miles an hour.

Conclusions.

I. The more the number of pairs you put the easier the work becomes.

II. On Dak the pair should be worked from 8 to 9 and in unavoidable circumstances 10 miles per hour.

III. The following spare harness parts should be sent:—

1 pair of traces.
1 pair of reins.

1 pair of pole straps.
2 Cotton ropes.
1 pair of Numdah* Pads (गुदका).

IV. Well-made good pairs should not be sent on Dak, but invariably those pairs which are rough and not thoroughly broken to harness and want a lot of work to make them steady and quiet ; for those stages where there are climbing up a long hill and going down a long descent and also in dangerous parts of the roads, you should have such pairs only as are thoroughly broken and on whom you could fully rely for the work you want them to do, or at the last stage where you finish your Dak by going through the town, you should have a well-put-together pair with complete harness.

V. Never give your best pairs on Daks to the indifferent drivers, but to the man only on whom you can rely and trust fully. In giving ordinary pairs to an indifferent coachman, if they are spoilt, you will not feel the same regret.

VI. Try to never send your best pairs on a long stage and on Daks as there is a likelihood of their not being looked after properly, by their being left to the sole mercy of the syces. But in unavoidable circumstances you can send your favourite pairs—say for a couple of hours—to the stage near your residence, *i.e.*, say about 8 to 10 miles from the place you are living in, so that after they have returned home you can look after them properly to your satisfaction.

Best time to travel by dak.

Whenever I had occasions of driving by Dak I always tried to keep up my time and avoided starting

* For use when a horse gets a sore-shoulder. It is very useful in the rainy season.

Putting the Pair on Dak.

in the middle of the day as it is very injurious to the animals. It has been found that the horses have dropped down dead on level roads within 6 miles from the starting point on account of apoplexy or sunstroke. It has been found best to start at an early hour, of the morning, say between 4 and 6 a.m., so that one can cover the early stages easily with a good pace, say 8 to 10 miles an hour as the morning breeze would keep the horses fresh and would not tire them out and at the same time one would reach his destination before noon. So it is very essential to start in the hot weather in the early mornings as the heat begins to tell from 10 a.m. In the hot weather I have always preferred to start either in the night after dinner, say from 9 p.m. onwards or in the early morning, as generally in this country one has not to go more than 50 miles. It is always better to send on the horses a day or two previous ahead to their respective stages, so that they may get rest at least over 24 hours; but in cases of emergency one cannot give so much rest to the horses on stages before they are worked. It is, however, very essential that they should get 6 hours' complete rest from the time they arrive at the stage and are again put to the carriage.

Dangers of night-driving.

In the rainy season it is better to start in the morning (or sometime in the day) and finish before it gets dark. In the monsoon the evenings get so very dark on account of clouds and rain that it becomes quite impossible to see anything a few yards further than the heads of the horses, and besides in this country the roads get so rough and muddy in the monsoon that it is quite impossible to distinguish whether you are on the road or on a side of it. The roads being narrow the lamps do not throw light further than a few paces on each side ot them, and even suppose they give you a good light, still in the rainy season it is very hard to distinguish the main part of the road from the other as the whole of the road gets muddy, and so you see exactly the same condition of the road all over until you come quite on the brink of the road, and then when you by the aid of your lamp see a ditch ("khad") on the same side, you have to turn the carriage to the opposite side and bring it on the main road. There is still another danger in night-driving in the monsoon and for which one has to be very careful, and that is the bullock carts and hired tongas (for public service) do not have lamps and that even if they have sometimes, the drivers will not light them until they have reached the Municipal limits; that their drivers, as a rule, are always found sleeping or drunk with the reins slipped, thus going at the mercy of their jaded and tired animals. The lot of saving them, therefore, falls on the shoulders of the coachman, who has not only to save his own carriage from running into them but has also to save the opposite conveyance from getting into collision with his own. In this connection I may just record an instance of an accident which Major F.G. Beville, I.A., C.I.E., Political Agent in Bhopawar, met while motoring at night in the month of November 1909. He said :— "* * * when on my way to Dhar from Mhow in a motor car with lights burning, I met a tonga without lights going in the same direction but on the wrong side of the road. The tonga was partly on the road, and consequently as there was ample room, I passed keeping to the left of the road, and as near the edge as possible. Along my edge of the road there was a long stack of metal. As I got close to the tonga the near-side pony jibbed and backed towards me and I found it quite impossible to get out of its way. It struck my motor on the off-side near the rear wheel breaking the wheel bracket, and the mud-guard and caused the tyre to burst.

I was going very slowly at the time and had for some distance previous to coming up to the tonga sounded both my horn and exhaust whistle. Immediately after the collision the driver of the tonga turned his ponies round, and whipped them up, evidently intending to run away in the hope that he may not be identified. However my Jamadar of Chaprassis who was with me managed to run after and stop the tonga . . . Not only was the damage to my motor due to the driver being on his wrong side, possibly asleep and not having his horses under control, but also to his attempt to drive off and leave me to my fate though I might, for all he knew, have been seriously injured as a result of his colliding with me."

In the monsoon one has to rely also on the sound o the wheels, so that when the carriage goes a little aside he may immediately know the difference between the sound of the wheels on the main road and of those going on the side, and thus he can bring the carriage on the main part within a few minutes.

Starting in the hot weather.

In the hot weather there is nothing more pleasant than starting in the night when it is quite cool and especially when you have a moonlight to drive with, and when such petty accidents could be avoided with ease and no special danger of their becoming serious ones is apprehended.

Pace.

In this country it has always been found advisable to keep one's pace from 8 to 9½ miles an hour in the cold and hot weather, while in the rainy season it is better to keep the pace from 7 to 8 miles an hour on an average.

Passengers and Luggage.

In driving a Dak great point for the consideration of the coachman is how many persons he should allow and how much luggage besides them he should have in his carriage. One cannot lay down a hard and fast rule in this matter, since it depends upon the local circumstances of the time. But generally it is better to take less luggage when the number of passengers is greater *and vice versa.* When the carriage is overloaded, certainly the coachman should not drive his horses at their usual pace, but he must drive them at a reduced pace. If the weight is lighter, then he can keep the usual pace. Whenever I had a full load I always kept my pace at the rate of 7 to 8 miles an hour on an average, and never exceeded. I may just make a remark here that there is no other better way for a beginner to gain his experience than to go on Dak and sit on the box by the side of an experienced coachman and watch his movements at every second, and if at times he does not understand a thing, he should immediately ask his tutor to explain to him the difficulty; so the beginner can pick up many things and get more new lessons daily, which would help him much in his study. There is also the question of the horses to be laid on Dak. I have come across many coachmen preferring to put quiet animals and made pairs on Dak; but I have always resented the idea.

Carriage with a Full Load.

Thorough pairs on special occasions.

The idea on the whole is not a bad one, but it should be worked on special occasions only, such as when ladies have to be driven and high personages, Royalties, etc., then only one is justified to lay the best of his pairs for the comfort of them whom naturally he does not like to see uncomfortable on the road ; but for ordinary Daks it is not essential at all.

Animals of different temperaments preferred.

It is always better to lay on Dak animals of different temperaments and even half-broken, as it gives sufficient time for coachmen to train them on the stages ; on the Dak a good coachman can give them good exercise and thus make them more quiet and amenable to their work in a short time. For the half-broken horses there is nothing better than to lay them on Dak, but entrust them to a good driver who can make them perfect within a very short time. It is no good to put on Dak a pair of unbroken animals ; nothing will improve them except separating them and putting them individually with made-up horses, who in time will be able to go together without any risk of getting spoilt.

The class of animal.

There are no other classes of animals I prefer for the Dak than (*a*) real good countrybred from Upper India which stand any amount of work, are hardy, strong and climatized to this country from the beginning, and (*b*) the Australian. The Australian horse is equally as strong and hardy an animal as a country-bred, but in the latter kind I have always preferred to get only that which is cast from an English battery, provided it is cast only for age, the reasons being that a battery horse is already found acclimatized to this country, and so there one does not run the risk of the climate affecting it, and also as long as it is on the active list of the battery it is kept quite fit by regular daily exercise. Secondly one naturally has not to pay a big sum for it; thirdly when the battery horse comes to the Native State it has not to work so hard and drag so heavy a load (a gun) behind it, but most probably only a light Victoria, Landau or a Wagonette. In short, it has a much lighter work to do in a Native State than in the battery. I can quote many instances where the casters have lasted as much as from 7 to 10 years without getting sick or sorry for a day. If they are properly looked after and cared for, there is no doubt that they will last as long as the period given above. This method is also very economical, since generally one has not to pay a high price for a Caster, and then after taking work for a couple of years if it dies or you are obliged to cast it, you need not worry, as your loss, if any, is trifling. Now there is another side of the question to be looked into—Why a young Australian is not better than a Caster? The answer to this question is that, generally there is a great risk run for over a year when the animal is bought from the Stables and till it gets acclimatized to the country. Secondly as long as the influences of climate of the country do not suit it, it does not get quite fit for the work. Thirdly you have to pay a higher price for it than for a Caster and then you cannot use it for hard and rough work till it gets quite fit for it, which takes more than a year and in some cases even still longer.

Now think for a moment if you buy four new pairs of Australians from the Stables and the price of each pair is, say, Rs. 1,200 at the minimum and then you have

Rest on a Stage.

to send those out on Dak. This would ruin them and make them totally unfit for any further work, with the result that you have either to cast them or sell them for whatever price they would fetch at the moment. To return therefore to our old question, *i.e.*, whether we are losers in such a concern or not: the answer to this question decidedly goes against us, because when we buy them we have to pay their full prices and within a couple of years when we cast them we cannot get even half of the price we had to pay for them. Then in addition to this many of the Native States have not generally got those facilities which the British Army has, such as properly looking after the new horses and taking that care of them which ought to be taken from the time they first arrive from a climate of a different part of the world till the climate of the place suits them,—I mean especially our lack exists in the Veterinary aid.

Veterinary aid.

We have to content ourselves in Native States with whatever aid we receive in this respect at the hands of either a Salotri or a Native Veterinary Surgeon—the latter so called because he goes through a prescribed course of training in some of the Veterinary Colleges established in some big cities of India, and thus by qualifying himself in the above Institute gets a degree of a graduate or so-called Veterinary Surgeon. But I am sorry to say that these Veterinary Surgeons have very little knowledge on the practical side, *i.e.*, they lack in experience, though they are quite up-to-date in the thesis of their science. In other words, they do not get as much practice to improve their knowledge as a Veterinary Surgeon of the Army Veterinary Corps would get; so the knowledge of the former gets by time rusted or limited. They do not get daily as many as 20 cases of different types of diseases. Are we therefore justified to ask our Native Veterinary Surgeons to be on the same level as that of the Army Veterinary Corps, whose experience cannot be denied? As for the Salotri,* it is getting quite scarce to secure a good hand in that line, who used to be easily obtainable 10 years ago.

Avoiding over-driving.

In driving the pairs on Dak the chief point to be remembered is that you should never take much work out of them so as to enable them to cover further journey if required beyond the stage where they are expected to have a change.

How to remedy unequal pace.

If the pair has not got equal pace or steps, then the pace should be kept according to the pace of the slower one or the latter will have to be galloped.

Driving with one horse, the other horse being dead.

While you are on the journey and by some unknown cause or reason one of the horses of the pair drops dead in harness and you have no means to reach the next stage, you must finish the stage with one horse only. There is not much to be altered in the way of harness, except putting a piece of rope through the pole-strap of the dead animal and tying it up tight to the bolt † of the splinter-bar ‡, which will keep the pole in its proper place. Secondly attach the coupling-reins of the dead animal to the bit of the horse in harness; thus the above method will enable you to reach the next stage.

* A native doctor who uses native medicines only.

† Muthia (मुठया.)

‡ Adia (आडया.)

Carriage to be drawn by one Horse.

Never put a pair of jibbers on Dak, but use a jibber with a strong and willing horse so that in case the former likes to jib the latter will not only allow it to have its own way but will drag him on till the jibber shares its work; so there will not be any possibility of your being left on the road.

Driving (on one side of the road) when the road is under repairs.

In the rainy season when the parts of the roads are under repairs, *i.e.*, when only the Moorum (metal) is spread and has not been rolled, you must drive the carriage on one side of the road and not in the middle *i.e.*, two wheels of either side of the carriage be kept out of the main part of the road on one side and if the part under repairs is of a long distance, then change sides of the road at your own judgment so as to distribute the work equally between the pair.

CHAPTER VIII.

Driving through the Town and in Processions.

Driving through the town.

WHEN going through the town it is essential that the driver should sit himself well in the "box." I do not mean by that, that he should on any account show off his abilities on the box by putting an extra coat of swagger in his position, but he should have the same natural position with a little more care. Secondly it is also necessary for him to drive his horses at a steady pace ; thus not only will they go collectedly and keep one pace but will give a good exhibition of their action to the eyes of the public. Nothing gives a worse spectacle than to see a horse in a pair galloping while the other—if he be an arrant slug—is dragged. There is also a very great advantage in driving horses at a steady pace, because if an unforeseen obstacle were to come, either the driver would manage to pull up his horses in time to save the accident or if he is too late to pull up, it will be easier for him to get clear of it by opening out his horses. Generally in small towns the children are allowed to play on the road and they have a habit of going across the road backwards and forwards before the coming vehicle, and while doing so in a fit of excitement, one of them loses his foot and down he comes on the ground, then it falls on the driver to save the child's life by either pulling up sharply or opening out his horses. The children, when they are in excitement, become quite deaf to the sound of the horn or even the shrieks of the coachman or the syces. On one occasion a child while running across the road lost his footing and came down about 1½ yards in front of my near-side horse ; naturally I could not pull up my horses ; even if I had tried to do so, I am sure the child would have been trodden on by one of the horses' fore-feet. Nothing was therefore left to me but to open out the pair and thus clear the child without touching it. I must say that the hair-breadth escape of this child was due simply to his good luck.

Driving in procession.

Before a procession starts the carriages are formed in rows. It is the duty of every coachman to watch the movements of the carriage next to him (on the right) and keep his horses ready to start as soon as the next carriage has taken a lead, thus forming into a line.

Signal of halt.

In going in procession the carriages have to be stopped and started every now and then ; and so it is essential that every coachman before pulling up should raise his whip so as to indicate to the coachman behind the signal of "Halt," which would prevent the running in of the pole of the carriage behind.

Nervous horse.

It is always better to have reliable horses in a procession and to avoid driving a nervous one specially, because at times slow going and the mere sight of the crowd of people make him nervous ; thus he will not only refuse to move an inch forward but will show his "defence" in every possible way he can, otherwise he may be a best Harness Horse. Even if we are doubtful of a certain animal in a pair, which although is well-matched in colour, it is better to leave him in the stall than drive him in the procession. If on the contrary we cannot find a match in colour for the other horse from any of the remaining horses, it is advisable that we match him with the one who is reliable though not of the same colour for the work we want him to do on the occasion.

CHAPTER IX.

BREAKING TO HARNESS.

HORSE-BREAKING is much the same subject as that of school-teaching. In Horse-breaking the theory is the same of all those concerned, but the difference only lies in the various methods adopted by individual breakers.

Objects of breaking.

The objects of the breaking are three in number. As Captain Hayes says in his book "Illustrated Horse-breaking" on page 29 (Chapter II), "the objects of horse-breaking are: (1) to make the animal quiet, both in and out of the stable; (2) to teach him to obey the orders of his rider or driver with promptness and precision; and (3) to establish in him the habit of applying his powers to the best advantage." It is obvious that all the endeavours and methods of breaking should be based on these objects.

Desirability of Early Training.

In Horse-breaking our first step should be towards early training, as (1) in young age the horse, so to speak, has no "vice" in himself; (2) the grasping power of the animal is found "pure" and "fresh;" and (3) his instincts of independence in opposition to the obedience of man are not so strongly developed as they would with age. In short, it can be said that education to young horses is not only more effective and impressive, but it would tend to make the animal a "Horse" early than late in life.

The cases "taken up" late in life will always stand, as far as the training is concerned, secondary to those taken up in early life. I may, therefore, define the approximate age for the commencement of training to be from 3 to 4 years, so that by the time the animal is "6 off" the whole part of the education in special subject (Driving) can be finished, and the animal may also be quite matured, the muscles so necessary for draught being well developed, to realise the benefits of the education it has received, and thus in its later years it will be able to utilize them in the best possible manner to his advantage.

The course of training.

The period of training should be about 3 years or at least not less than 2 years, in which time a thorough breaker should be able to get his pupil passed out of the course of training, *viz* :—

(1) 1st year : schooling on foot with long reins.

(2) 2nd year : driving the novice in harness with and old horse.

(3) 3rd year ; driving the pair together.

In giving lessons to the novice it should always be remembered that the breaker should on no account push the lessons one after another into his pupil's head until he is thoroughly satisfied that the pupil has completely understood and grasped one. After he has been so satisfied he should proceed to give him the next one. By giving too many lessons at a time it would only mean to muddle the head of the novice, making him unable to progress in training steadily.

Principles of breaking.

In successful breaking, four principles are very essential for the breaker to remember, *viz*:—(1) application of proper punishment and reward; (2) non-interruption in the lesson; (3) the lesson should on no account be terminated, by reason of the instincts of independence of the horse, in direct opposition to the obedience to the breaker; and (4) the establishment of mutual confidence between the breaker and the novice, which is the chief principle of, and the whole key to, successful breaking.

Quieting a new Horse.

When a pupil first comes as 3 years old to the stables, the first step of the breaker would be to make him 'quiet' and 'gentle.' The best method to be adopted in this direction that I can recommend, is of Captain Hayes* called the "Head and Tail Method," which is as follows :—

"Having put a head-stall on the horse, tie one end of a rope or cord by a double sheet bend to his tail, draw the head about a third of the way round and tie the free end of the rope to the head-stall, so that the head may be kept in this position. The longer the tail, the thicker may be the rope; and the rope or cord should be so fixed to the head-stall that it can be readily loosened or tightened. I have found that it is a great improvement to attach a short rope or strap (a stirrup leather will do) to the other side of the head-stall (away from which the horse's head is turned) so that

* *Vide* pp. 156 to 158 of "Illustrated Horse-breaking."

the operator may catch it and thus stop the revolving horse, when he sees that the animal is getting giddy and in danger of falling. To begin with, the length of the cord which connects the head and tail should be so regulated, that it will be just sufficient to make the animal turn round without being able to go forward. In order to obtain increased control, the cord should be gradually tightened from time to time, according as the pupil becomes accustomed to the movement; but on no account to such an extent as would cause him to be in danger of falling down; for, our object here is to avoid giving him just reason for alarm. Besides, a fall, when the animal is in this position, is not without danger to neck or back."

What to do when the Animal has been fixed.

"When the horse has been fixed up in this manner, we may begin operations by gently cracking a whip while standing a few yards away from him, and may continue to do so, if he expresses impatience or alarm by going round and round, until he pays no attention to the noise made by the whip, although we may crack it all over him. We should gradually shorten the cord which connects his head to his tail, and, at the same time, should continue to approach nearer to him, and to increase the noise of the cracking of the whip. Out of hundreds of "nervous" horses which have passed through my hands, I have never seen a single one which, by this "head and tail" plan, would not, within an hour at the outside, allow the whip to be cracked all over him without evincing the slightest fear, even when the connecting cord had been removed from the head-stall and tail. While using the whip in the manner described, we should carefully refrain from hitting the animal with it.

After the pupil has lost all fear of the whip, we may proceed in a similar manner to make him bear, without flinching, being touched with a long pole of convenient thickness and weight."

Touching the Animal with pole.

"We should begin by placing the pole on the least sensitive part of his body (his "crest", on which the mane grows), and should work up by degrees to the more ticklish ones, such as under the belly, down the legs, in front, behind, and between them. In this way we should go over the whole of the animal's body with the pole."

Flourishing a pole with cloth attached to one end.

"When he submits to be touched all over, we may try the effect of noise on him, as, for instance, that produced by beating an empty paraffin oil tin, and we may finally endeavour to frighten him by flourishing in front of, and all over him, a white banner or some other cloth fixed to the end of the pole. In doing all this, our object should be to make him go round as much as possible, by startling him, though without hurting him in the slightest; for the more trying will have been his experience, the less likely will he subsequently be to become startled at anything unusual happening. When he has thoroughly given in, the cord may be taken off his head and tail."

Besides this there are other methods too for the purpose, but they require much longer time. If the novice is quite raw, he may be put into a "wooden box" (अरगडा) and by putting him there, he will be quite helpless to show any sign of fright at the time when he is to be made "gentle" and "quiet." Thus the breaker can get all over his body with safety to himself. In "gentling" the novice our chief aim should be always not to create fear of the human being in him. Our whole success lies in this fact. The "box" also can be used when the harness is to be put on the animal for the first time.

I would suggest that the process of "gentling" and "quieting" the novice, if properly practised, should be finished in or about the end of the first week.

Harnessing the horse for the first time.

When the novice has once become sufficiently "gentle" and "quiet", we should proceed to put an unjointed or rubber-mouth snaffle on him and the driving-pad or "Dumb-jockey." At this stage it will not be difficult for us to put the gear on; but if he were to show any sign of fear from the gear, it would be advisable to put him into the "box" and then there he should be harnessed; after being harnessed the novice should be kept loose in his stall with the gear on, for about a couple of hours daily, both in the mornings and evenings, till we find that he has become sufficiently docile with the gear.

SCHOOLING.

Driving on foot with long reins.

Before giving this exercise to the novice it is very essential to have an enclosed *manège*, so as to get him to pay more attention to his work, as in an enclosed *manège* the novice will have very little opportunity to divert his attention to other things than in an open ground.

Sudden Collapse of the Back Axle.

Time of exercise.

The cold weather (from about the last week of September to the first week of March) is the best time to work. In this season the breaker can, without any interruption, attend to his work daily. The time for exercising the novice is from 7 a. m. to 8-30 a. m., and in the evening from 4-30 p. m. to 6 p.m. I do not, however, mean here in the least that the breaker should always stick to this period actually, but I entirely leave the points to his own discretion and judgment of the (1) circumstances of the locality, and (2) the condition of his pupil. In the hot weather the breaker cannot get on with his work properly owing to the excessive heat, while in the rainy season, *i.e.*, from the last week of June to the last week of September it is practically impossible to attend to the work regularly.

Driving with single rein.

When the novice is led to the *manège* withhis breaking gear on, the first lesson he should receive is that of circling with one rein: if the breaker would like to circle him on the left, the breaker should pass the off-rein through the near-ring of snaffle, while in the case of circling to the right he should pass the near rein through off-ring of snaffle. It is very necessary to have the knee caps put on the novice for the school work, as they would protect his knees if he were to come down, care being taken that they are not put on too tight whereby the horse may be rubbed or too loose whereby they may slip down and so bring the horse down. In circling the animal whichever side, care should be taken that he is circled with "light hands," or it is very likely that the novice might begin to hang on one rein more than on the other. The novice should not be put in the beginning on a "short circle," but on a fairly big one. At the start the novice should be made to "walk" his circle with the words of command, which should always be given in a long voice of "walk," "trot" or "canter." At the same moment the breaker should slightly "feel" his mouth with his rein and "click" to him or "show" him the breaking whip, so as to negotiate the order to the mind of the novice to start. In like manner at the time of stopping, the word "halt" should be used in a longer voice than that of the previous ones. When the animal has finished his first circle and is at the "halt" the breaker should bring the novice to him and pat him on the neck to indicate his appreciation of his work, also frequently giving him as a reward one or two stalks of lucerne grass which should be carried between the belt and the trousers at the breaker's back. Then the breaker should put his novice on to the next circle. These lessons of circling with single rein should not take more than a fortnight.

Driving with double reins.

In driving with double reins we must pass the reins through the "rein-bearers" and fix the ends to the rings of snaffle. We must then put the novice on either of the circles at "walk" and make him change the circle with the aid of these reins. At the time of changing the circle, give the word "change" in a sharp voice and "feel" the "outward rein" of the animal till he changes round the circle. We must have these lessons well practiced at the "walk" before we proceed to the "trot" or "canter." In changing the circle the breaker should always take care that the novice changes his required fore-leg at the correct moment and also keeps it in the right place, while he is on circle. In this connection I may just give a hint* to the breaker with regard to his position at the time of changing the circle :—

"To do this, both the reins should be taken in the left hand with at least a yard of slack. Then sliding the right hand well forward on the right rein and taking a long pace forward with the right foot to enable the right hand to get a good reach forward, the right rein is drawn tight to turn the pony's head to the right, and the left rein coming against the pony's flanks makes him change his legs behind."

In circling the novice the breaker should keep the inward rein so short as would enable him to see the inward eye of the horse the whole time while he is on circle. If the novice is found to be carrying his head rather low, the use of "single" bearing-rein will be indispensable. In this connection I would refer to the following lines from Captain Haye's Book on Horse-breaking (*vide* pp. 169-170):—

"The bearing-rein has a nose-band which comes under the lower jaw, in the chin-groove, below the mouthpiece of the snaffle, and is connected to the bearing-rein by a strap running down the centre of the face. The bearing-rein can be fixed to the driving-pad or saddle. This form of bearing-rein keeps the head up by acting on the chin-groove, the bony surface of which is smooth and rounded. As it in no way interferes with the mouth, it is much superior to the ordinary kind, which raises the head by pressing on the corners of the mouth."

In the same manner if the novice is found raising his head, standing martingale be made use of. In school-

---

* *Vide* page 64 of Col. De Lisle's Book "Polo in India."

ing I would recommend the breaker to keep the pace of the animal as much as he can at the "trot." It is obvious that the training we are giving the animal is for harness and not for any other work, and so it is very essential for a carriage-horse to go at "trot" than at "canter." In other words, we must discourage going at "canter" as far as possible.

In schooling, the work should generally be to (*a*) draw a circle, (*b*) draw a long figure of eight, (*c*) halt, (*d*) turn about, (*e*) rein back, (*f*) spiral, and (*g*) figure of eight. All these lessons go to tend the animal handy at shoulders and flanks, and light at mouth. If the art of changing the circle from one to another has been mastered, the breaker will find that he can stand in one position in the *manège* and make his novice go round him in circles and figures of eight, etc., at fast trot.

Breaking to the carriage.

In the training of the second year's course the breaker should sufficiently finish his work of schooling with the novice and be prepared to drive him with an old brake-horse. In putting the novice we must put the brake-horse first and then the novice. Generally, I would recommend to my readers to put the young animal on the near-side first, as it is found from experience that the driver can have a better control on the near-side. Later on we can change the novice, if we require him to work on the off-side.

I do not propose to repeat here what precautions are essential to be taken at the time when the novice is to be put to the carriage, as I have already described them in para. III of the Chapter II. When the novice is put to the carriage and found ready to start, we should first touch our brake-horse with the whip or give "click" to him, and at the same time, only "feel" the novice's mouth, which will negotiate the command of "starting" to him. It is quite possible that the novice may not be able to start the carriage in the beginning; so we must make the brake-horse do this job, and also have the novice dragged for a few paces on; if this is practised, I am sure it will not make the young animal frightened of his work and lose heart, but will on the other hand create "the art of starting" the carriage in him. When we have once got on well with the course, we should gradually make the novice to work by simply cracking the whip on his near-side, if he be on that side and *vice versa.* But great care should be taken that we do not touch any of his part with the whip. We should only drive the young horse for a few days in the "*Maidan*" (open place), where he should be practised for a time on his old school lessons. In the beginning we should invariably avoid driving him on the road, till we find that he obeys our orders on the "Maidan" on both the reins with precision. Then we can proceed to drive him on the road (outside the town). The novice should not however be driven for a long while, *i.e.*, his early lessons should be short and the distances short also. We must very gradually work him up to this by steady driving. Care should be taken to see that he keeps his paces well, carries himself well up and does not try to break into canter or hang on his bit, or keep himself behind the bit. In this way the novice should be driven regularly. In the end of this course, *i.e.*, before putting him together with his comrade, the novice should be driven both in the day-light and night through the town with the brake-horse, so as to accustom him to the things to which he might be liable to come across.

Thus at the time of the commencement of the third year course, by breaking the pair of colts separately and driving them individually with old brake-horses, we should be able to put and drive them together. In driving them together, only care will have to be taken that they keep their paces equal and distribute the work equally.

Before closing this Chapter I would request my readers to pay their special attention to the fact that it is very desirable and essential that the breaking of young animals is entrusted to one driver or breaker from the beginning to the end, and should on no account be allowed to be made a mess by allowing others to put their fingers in, which may be condensed in the old saying " too many cooks spoil the broth."

CHAPTER X.

Tonga Driving.

Tonga.

THE Tonga is a two-wheeled vehicle used specially for " kutcha " (unmetalled) or rough road in the district, generally with a pair of ponies and is a convenient and comfortable means to travel in the country.

Harness.

The harness is the same as that of double harness, the only main difference being that on the top of the pads it has rollers on which the bar rests ; thus the action of the bar is worked freely from one side to another. The roller-bolts and leather straps should be of very strong material as the weight of the Tonga generally rests on them. The traces used for the Tonga are of the same style as that of single-harness.

In India a light extra iron-bar is attached to the bits inside between the ponies, so as to keep them separate as on the rough road (kutcha), the ponies by being kept on their paths are able to drag the Tonga in an easier and better way than otherwise.

Holding the reins and driving.

The holding of the reins and the general method of driving a Tonga are the same as that of double harness with the left, but one has sometimes to hold the reins in both the hands while driving on the " kutcha " road.

Tonga ponies.

Country-bred ponies and mules are generally preferred for the Tonga work. The height of the ponies generally should be 14 hands or thereabout.

Breaking.

It is always better to break a pair of Tonga ponies first in double-harness with a brake horse before driving them together in a Tonga.

Winner in Mhow Horse Show in 1907.

CHAPTER XI.

Hints to Beginners.

WHEN you wish to learn to drive, always mean to become a good coachman. To reach this aim you should try to drive with an experienced whip and follow the principles which have been laid down after many years' experience.

When you are on the "box," always remember that you are the Captain of a ship, and you should be the last person to leave it in the time of danger, as the safety of the passengers lies with you.

Always try to drive to the comfort of your passengers.

Experientia docet.—If you spend half a century in driving, still you will find that you have something to learn.

CHAPTER XII.

HORSE AND HIS VICES.

Nothing in this world is perfect that draws breath,
  Nothing in this world is certain except death.
For nought so vile that on the earth doth live,
But to the earth some special good doth give;
Nor aught so good, but, strained from that fair use,
Revolts from true birth, stumbling on abuse;
Virtue itself turns vice, being misapplied,
And vice sometimes by action dignified.
        (*Romeo and Juliet*, *Act* 2, *s*. 3).

General.

IT will not be out of place for me to mention here that the "Horse" is as much a "mortal being" as a "man." I am sure the readers will agree with my views that the above fact is universally established, and also that no animal kingdom (mortal) in this universe is "Perfect" except the Providence, and so it is only our fancy when we say that a certain phenomenon is good or bad. If we find more virtues in an animal than the evils, we call him good and *vice versa;* nothing is bad in this universe but that it simply depends upon the fact how it suits one's purpose, it being quite immaterial whether it relates to the human race or the animal. The development of vice in youth much depends upon the association, because much can be gained through the medium of good association and on the contrary much can be lost by the influences of evil one; so it is an established fact that it is as easy to train a "green" colt as to train a young baby, because in tender or young age of any of the animal kingdom no drop of evil can be found, but it is generally full of innocence. The novice may develop evil habits as he begins to grow, if he is surrounded with unhealthy company, simply because in young age he has not the capacity of reasoning out which is good or bad, and the novice through his mere innocence may begin to cultivate or adopt the evils of his unhealthy association, and later on as he grows may 'take' them in himself, and then when he once takes them and sticks to them, he becomes a spoilt child; so it is constantly said that it is easy to train or coach a novice than to train a spoilt child. In this connection two questions may be asked, *viz.*, why it is easier to train a young novice than a spoilt child and secondly, why it is difficult to train a spoilt novice. The answer to the first question does not require much explanation, because it has already been stated above that when the body is pure of all evils anything that you wish to assimilate with it can take its natural course easily in its circulation, as there is no drop of evil or foreign matter inserted so as to oppose it except "good" or innocence. The answer to the second question is also very much the same, that is, when a novice has once taken in himself nothing but evils through the medium of evil association, it falls on the trainer to perform a double duty, that is, the latter has to take away all the evils first which have been absorbed in the veins of his novice and then when the novice once becomes quite free of this long-timed evil disease, the trainer may be able to create "good" in him. It is in the beginning just the same to say that "prevention is better than cure."

Even now our chief point is not cleared, *viz.*, what we mean by the term "vice in a Horse." It is a well-known fact that Nature has given to every creature of its universe—from an insect to a man—the instinct of self-preservation against a power superior to itself. Now we must see what are the means of self-preservation given to the Horse. Chiefly they are two in number, *viz.*, kicking and biting,—which is to be found in almost all the quadruped animals also. Under these circumstances, we cannot draw the inference and call them the "deliberate" vices; but we must on the contrary call them the gifts of Nature given to this noble creature for self-preservation, as the so-called vice in a Horse is as a rule "a manifestation of his instinct of self-preservation and has nothing to say to innate turpitude" (*vide* page 24 of Captain Hayes' Book on "Horse-Breaking)." But when the horse makes a "habit" and practises them "for the gratification of his own ends, in direct opposition to the well-understood and legitimate orders of man, and those which prompt him to make unprovoked and hostile attacks on man or other animals," it is to be called a deliberate vice.

The nervous vice in a horse is due either to his shyness or unfounded fear of his surroundings or active hostility or to resist control.

Thus we can say in short that there are two chief kinds of vices in the Horse, *viz.*, deliberate and nervous. Now I must come to the material phase of facts of the chapter.

Kicking.

The course of Nature is the art of God.
(*Night Thoughts* "9", *line 1267*).

This vice is established in a horse chiefly through the following causes, *viz.*, (1) ill-treatment at the hands of his trainer; (2) some parts of the harness not fitting, but on the contrary causing irritation to some parts of the body of the animal; and (3) carelessness at both the times while putting the harness on and putting him to the carriage or taking him out of the carriage.

If proper care is taken on all such occasions, I very much doubt the animal will ever get into this vice as long as he is a harness horse.

The principal sign of a kicker is that just before he actually commences to kick he will waggle or twist his tail and put his ears back, and if the coachman is clever enough to judge he will at once divert the mind of the animal by giving a couple of smart cuts on his neck and also by "playing" well with his mouth, so that once the mind of the animal is diverted he would not be able to think for the time being of kicking; the trap could thus be saved from being smashed.

It is always advisable to put the pole strap of a kicker tight to keep the animal well up to its collar and also to "play" with his mouth, so as to prevent him from planning out his attack. But if he were to kick, in spite of all these precautions, then only at that moment punish him severely by giving him good cuts across the loins through the "flanks." This form of punishment, I find, is very severe, and makes an immediate effect on the novice, if applied in time only when the hind legs of the animal *are off the ground*. In support of this, I may quote an authority here:— "If a horse which kicks receives punishment when his hind legs are off the ground, he will remember that he got hurt for kicking. If, on the contrary, the punishment is received after his hind legs have come down, he will be unable to connect in his mind the ideas of these two facts. . . . But if the kicking is a vice, we ought to severely correct him the moment it is practised, and to prevent it we should forcibly raise his head and neck in order to put the weight on his hind quarters" (*Vide* "Breaking and Riding" by James Fillis, page 9.)

Again at this stage I may quote two methods suggested by Captain Hayes for the prevention of kicking :—

(1) "An excellent method* of curing or preventing the practice of kicking in harness is to attach, at each side, a rope or rein to the crupper, say, four or five inches from the dock, pass it through a pulley or ring on the shaft, at about right angles with the point of attachment to the crupper ; carry it forward and fix it to the ring of the snaffle, at such a length that, if the horse tries to kick, he will give his lower jaw a violent blow. While acting as a kicking strap, it will be the means of making the horse associate in his mind the idea of pain with kicking in harness."

(2) "The old expedient of tying a kicker's tail to the splinter-bar is often successful in breaking the animal of his vice."

The use of bearing rein is also a very invaluable method of preventing the animal from kicking ; if it is properly put, the moment the animal tries to put his head down before bringing up his hind quarters, it will not only pinch his upper jaw but will oblige him to raise his head, and when once his head is well up, it will be impossible for him to raise his hind quarters to kick, as the weight would fall on them.

* "Horse-Breaking" by Capt. Hayes, pages 333 and 334.

From the methods suggested and cited above, I hope my readers will realise that the application of these methods prove the fact that: *to prevent the animal from kicking, the only solution is to raise his head and neck, and thus put the weight on his hind quarters.*

Getting the tail over the rein and kicking when in harness.

Along with the vice of kicking, some animals have the habit of getting their tail over the rein and kicking while they are in harness. For this vice I can suggest no other remedy, as it is found in very rare cases, except only that the driver ought to keep a strict eye on the movements of the tail of the animal, who, when found waggling his tail with the idea of getting it over the rein, the driver should instantaneously raise the rein up so high that the tail of the animal cannot reach it and at the same moment should "feel" the horse's mouth well and also give a couple of smart cuts on the neck of the horse. This practice will in time be found itself a cure for this vice.

Rearing.

Rearing is the first or mild form of jibbing. This vice is found among young animals and especially with those who are of excitable temper. If proper care is not taken of this vice in the beginning, there is much danger of its being turned into jibbing. The young animals, who are of excitable and impatient nature and who resent the idea of being kept in the same position, develop this vice. The cure for this vice is only to make the animal "steady," and he should be regularly driven with an old break horse and should also be made to stand when he is put to the trap for a while before starting. In other words, the trainer should not try to start away immediately the animal is put to the trap.

Jibbing.

Jibbing is an acute stage or obstinate form of rearing. The most appropriate definition I find is of Captain Hayes, (*vide* his book on "Horse Breaking," page 309) who says "a jibber is a horse which without just cause, refuses to proceed in any required direction, although he may be willing to go in some other direction. As a rule, a jibber will turn to one side, but not to the other."

In curing this vice our first object should be to overcome his obstinacy, and gradually we must work him up to obey our orders. The jibber should know at all costs that we are not going to be led away by his obstinate whims, but that he is to obey our orders. Secondly, the moment he begins to practise this form of "obstinate defence" he should receive punishment with such severity as to the proportion of the offence.

The jibber will always stand in the harness with his fore-legs well forward, and thus he will bring the collar on his neck instead of allowing it to be rested against his shoulders; in other words, the jibber will avoid, as much as he can, to "stand up to his collar."

To cure this vice our first step should be towards putting the "Breeching" on the jibber, which will prevent him from hanging back and knocking against the splinter bar. Secondly, we should pole him quite loose, which will oblige him to "stand up to his collar." Thirdly, we should drive the jibber "with a horse bigger and stronger than himself, who will fairly drag the refractory animal along" [*vide* page 67 "The

Carriage-horse" by Earl of Onslow, Badminton Library Series (Driving)]. Another method is to put a rope under the jibber's tail and pull him along; a third one I have known successful is to put a running cord through his nose-band, drag his head to that of the other horse and start the other horse. There is also one more method and that is to run a rope or cord through one of the fore-legs of the jibber, at the same time making the old horse start.

From my own experience I can say that with this method I had been successful in curing 75 per cent. cases of this vice. No doubt, on the other hand, I must admit that this method not only takes a very long time to cure this vice but it requires very careful driving and prompt judgment of the coachman.

If a pair jibb, it is always better to break them of the vice separately before driving them together.

Pulling away and hanging against the pole when in double harness.

To find any of these two vices in a horse, is a sign due to his being "over-driven." In rectifying either of these vices the aim should be not to over-work the animal. For both of these vices, it is very essential for one to alter the coupling-reins according to his own judgment of the circumstances. Secondly it is also necessary to "flick" the animal for the former vice on the outer part of his neck and shoulder, and for the latter on the inner part of his neck and shoulder. Cases where this vice has become a habit, I have seen cured by strapping an old dandy brush inwards to the pole. In the case of hanging on the pole, some other prickly substance such as a small piece of gorst cut from a bush, can bé used and *vice versa* in the case of pulling away from the pole

Shying.

Shying in a horse is due mainly to the following causes :—

(1) Natural timidity, (2) Nervousness and (3) Fear. In curing this vice, we ought to treat the animal first very "gently." When a horse shies of a certain object, our first duty would be to make him accustom to that object of which he is afraid. If, on the contrary, again he were still to have "nonsense" in him, then it is very essential that we should punish and correct him smartly on the spot, so that he may well remember in his mind the fault for which he has been awarded punishment: but I always prefer to show him the object several times and to coax him about it. I am not a believer in the whip for a horse who shies; I believe in the voice, and that a horse punished for shying is liable to be more frightened when he passes the object again. The only time to punish a horse for shying is when he does so for mere "devilment," which is not often the case and depends on a horse's temperament.

Plunging forward when starting in harness.

It is purely a sign of impatience, nervousness and excitable temper in a horse. It is only practised by a horse in harness, when he is full of teens and has not had enough work to do. In curing this vice we must exercise him daily with steady work and also by making him "gentle" in harness, so that he may gain "confidence" in his work. But care should be taken that on no account undue haste is exercised in curing the vice as there is every possibility of its being turned into "Rearing."

Prancing while (going) in harness.

It is practised by a horse only when he is fresh, refrains from doing the work and keeps himself " behind the bit." The vice can be cured by regular steady driving, making him do the work and keeping him to its bit. It is only a matter of time.

Savaging or Biting.

The horse is said to " savage " only when he makes use of his teeth as an instrument of aggression. This vice is very difficult to cure, but as a preventive measure we might use the leather or net muzzle while driving him, or have a leading rein fastened from his bridle to the other side of the pad long enough for him to answer the rein, but short enough to prevent his being able to reach the other horse.

CHAPTER XIII.

BITTING.

THIS is one of the most important subjects which concerns the training of the horse-flesh. If the use of this art is not properly made, it is pretty sure that the life of the horse is ruined for ever. Everything that concerns the training of the novice depends upon it. The Bit is the only medium through which the wishes of the driver are conveyed to the brains of the horse and should not be considered as an instrument used for the only purpose to stop the horse by sheer force.

I, therefore, deem it necessary to give this subject a special place in this Book. It is only by experience, constant observation and trial that we can find the best bit for the horse, because it has been proved that the horses go better in one bit than in another. In other words, we should never put pressure on the reins or balance our seat on the "box" by means of putting the pressure of the body on the reins. I am sorry to say that this tendency of balancing on the reins when on the "box" is found among the majority of native coachmen. Nothing will injure more the mouth of the horse than by constantly "hanging" on it; so, in short, I may say here that we should "play" with his mouth, and when we want him to go to some required direction should "feel" his mouth.

Four-in-hand-Snaffles.

Therefore in bitting the animal we should make the use of the most mild bit in the beginning, so as to avoid giving him a "hard" mouth. Generally in driving the Liverpool Bit is used, but I would prefer to have an Indian-Rubber Snaffle in the beginning for the use of the novice, and then in later period we should change it into double ring Wilson Snaffle, and then in the third period we should put him to the curb, *i.e.*, Liverpool Bit. The reason of the changes in the bit is only that when the novice has completed his training he might be required to go as a leader in the Tandem or Four-in-hand or in the wheel ; so it is very essential that we should put him in curb rather than in snaffle, as it is always risky to drive a Tandem or Four-in-hand in snaffles, though the horses might possess good mouths. Even in pair, I would say that it is essential that we should drive them in curb than in snaffle. It is just the same to drive a horse in snaffle or in Liverpool Bit, the only difference being as to how the reins are fixed to the latter bit. From experience it is found that a driver feels the same amount of weight of the horses' mouth when they are driven in Liverpool Bit with reins fixed with the port or in big rings, as when they are in snaffle. The signs of bad mouth can be visible or felt when a driver has to fix his reins in the *last hole* of the Bit with curb chain tight. It can be said that the horses possess medium or fair mouths, when they have to be driven by fixing the reins in the middle hole.

Faults of mouth.

Along with this it is just as well to treat the subject of faults of mouth. This vice is created simply on account of bad hands and too much pressure on the reins or constant "hanging" on the mouth of the horse. These faults are chiefly two in number, *viz.*, (1) Pulling and (2) Boring.

Pulling.

The horse is said to pull when he practises this vice in his defence from a spirit of sheer defiance to the wishes of his driver. The cure for this is only a question of time. Though there are several kinds of bits to be made use of, they are not a permanent cure; no doubt by their appliance an immediate effect would be produced, but it will be only a temporary relief, because the cause does not lie with the mouth alone but it chiefly lies in the brain. We should therefore try to root it out from his brain instead of wasting time in applying the bits of severe type. The general causes of pulling are due to the (1) hot-headedness, (2) excitement, (3) injuries to the mouth, and (4) bad bitting.

When a horse begins to show a sign of the first two causes, he should be at once taken to the school and be given a sharp lesson in circle, turn and rein-back with double reins on foot and with the snaffle on. The work he should receive must be hard, *i.e.*, he should be worked daily for an hour or so and be kept the whole time on "canter." After finishing the school work he should be put with a brake-horse and be driven regularly with care and steadiness. I am sure with this process in time, the puller will "give up his nonsense" and become a quiet harness horse again.

If the horse be found injured in his mouth, he should be given complete rest until his injuries are cured and then put in the school again, as stated above.

Secondly, if the cause lies in the bad bitting, it should be rectified at once.

Boring.

The horse is said to bore against the bit when he carries his head too low and brings his chin to his breast. In some cases, where this vice has been confirmed, I have noticed the horses bringing their heads so low down and bending their necks to the extent that their cheeks of the bit are in contact with the breast; the more the driver pulls at the bit, the less will it act on their mouths.

The remedy for this is to put the horse into the school again and give him sharp lessons in circle, rein-back and turn with long reins, with the snaffle and the bearing reins on, which will make the horse raise his neck in a correct position. But when thus driving the animal of this vice with a brake-horse, it is very essential that the driver sticks to and adopts the principle of "give and take." There are coachmen who make all the horses they ever drive bore, but I have always found if they have not been driven by them for a very long time, a week's regular driving in a brake with bearing reins will put them right again.

When a horse bores on one rein more than the other, we may follow the same course as stated above. But more attention should be paid mainly to getting him to turn to the side on which he actually bores, so long as he does not easily turn to it as to the other.

CHAPTER XIV.

MISCELLANEOUS.

The Turn-out of an old-typed Gentleman.

IT is certainly worth while to give a chapter to this native idea prevalent amongst the old country gentlemen in order to know what idea the native people possess of driving and value of the horse-flesh in this era. Generally they have the tendency of imitating more than of acquiring the knowledge in its true form. Very often we see on an old-fashioned turn-out, a man sitting on the " box " somehow having not the least idea of his position and knowing not what to do when he is there ; the reason for this is not far to look at, as the so-called coachman is in reality something else. He may have been employed as a dressing-boy or a cook's mate, etc., in the house of the gentleman who, in many cases, being given to false economy, likes to get two birds shot with one stone. Then are we justified in calling that man who sits on the box, a driver or a coachman ? No. We may term him by saying that he is everything and nothing, only getting a low salary—not even Rs. 6 per month. Is it ever possible that a servant who is a cook's mate, dressing-boy, syce as well as a driver can attend to all these multifarious duties properly ? Surely not. However a clever chap he may be, he will not find time to look after all these various offices satisfactorily.

Harness.

The harness is never cleaned or touched and many of the main parts get completely destroyed or fall gradually to pieces. If a slight repair is occasionally wanted to a particular part, it is not only not attended to at once but is left till that part completely breaks down. If even the harness was to be touched for a slight repair, the owner will be quite content to have it put together by tying it up with a piece of thread or string.

The fact of not cleaning the harness does not only look bad to the public but is injurious to the animal and it inflicts cut all over the shoulder.

Horse.

The non-attendance of the driver or the syce—there being no particular servant responsible for its management, bad feeding—a horse of 15 hands getting 3 seers of gram (equivalent to 6 lbs.) and 30 poolas of grass per diem—and this too only if the man in charge of the horse is an honest fellow,—the every day neglect in giving him his feed and water at regular times the animals being left without grass for days and the neglect of grooming—from all this I leave it to my readers to judge for themselves the lamentable condition of the poor jaded animal, whom the tyranny of fates have destined to be in the hands of such a merciless owner—and who after a half-starved life of labour being left to shift for himself so lank and weak, becomes the helpless spectator of his own deceased skeleton.

Carriage.

The carriage too of such an owner, which is handed down to him from one generation to another and in which he takes pride as his most valued heir loom, is not less repulsive than the harness or the jaded horse pictured above. With the linings lying out, paint all faint, shutters reclining out of their sockets and wheels running at obtuse angle to the axle, it is for my readers to conceive whether it is fit to call such a turn-out a carriage or a trap in its true sense. If the owner of such a vehicle were questioned as to why he does not get it put right or get rid of it, the reply is that he could not afford to do so and without it, his position would be degraded. Then what is the use of glorifying in the possession of such a rickety carriage with a jaded horse when he could not afford their proper up-keep? Is it humiliating to him to keep a decent trap rather than such an unseemly vehicle? Could he not do with a good decent Tonga with a pair of 14-hand ponies? But alas! the shallow pride has too strong a hold on his vain mind to allow him to change the trap to a Tonga; for he thinks that the show that he presents to the outside public by driving in a carriage, a sorry spectacle, or however rickety it be—is more conducive to his respectability than if he were to drive in a Tonga.

Native Coachman or Driver.

As a rule they are men more of a practical side than of anything else. Some of them who have experience at the back are seen to possess very good nerves. It is proved that those who have been first employed as syces and have worked for years mostly under experienced drivers have in the end turned out to be good coachmen, but when they come to this stage they require more practice in actual driving than anything else and such by driving with experienced hands they soon pick up. But I should say that these are very exceptional and rare cases. I have found that only those native coachmen who have experience and iron nerves could break and drive a most vicious type of an animal with ease and comfort and carry out orders with precision. In short, *a native coachman is nothing but a creature of practice.*

The following passage of the famous authority—the noble writer, I mean His Grace the Duke of Beaufort, which I am quoting here will, I hope, be sufficient to enable my readers to form an idea as to what in India a native driver is like (*vide* pp. 3 to 5 of the Book on "Driving" of the Badminton Library Series, Chap.):—

"That dreadful sight, which is to be seen a hundred and more times every day in the streets of London, of gentlemen and their coachman (gardeners, I ought to say) driving one or a pair with their hands close up to their noses, and a rein in each hand, the two hands being from six to twelve inches apart, is enough to give anyone, with the least notion of how a man should drive, a fit of the shivers."

"Watch them! See the man with the gold hat-band, with a very long crop to his whip, light-coloured with dark knots, all the way up, and at the end of his thong a red whipcord lash (horror!)—see him fetched old brougham horse one from his ear to his high goose rump. Mark the effect! The off rein being held with the whip in the right hand, there comes suddenly two feet of slack on that train. Our poor friend the brougham horse having received this vicious cut, being still held by the near rein, and not having his mouth touched by the off one, makes a dart to the near side, and either knocks a lamp-post with his fore-wheel, runs into the dust-cart standing by the curb-stone, or is saved from this calamity by a frightful scramble and exertion on the part of the personage with a gravel walk round his hat. See, again, a few yards further on, the gentleman driving himself in a·phæton with his hands up close to his nose. The omnibus in front of him pulls up short: our friend must do the same. He has reins in both hands instead of only in his left hand, in which latter case he would simply catch hold of his reins behind his left hand with his right hand, shortening them quickly and at once, and pull his horse or pair of horses up with the left hand. Being, however, in the same position as the coachman of the brougham, we have just seen what does he do? The only thing possible. His hands go up above the top of his hat. But that does not stop his horses, and he leans back and back and back still more. What is the matter with the poor gentleman? Is he in a fit? Or does he wish to shake hands with the groom sitting behind him? Or is there a balloon passing over-head that he wishes to see?"

My recollections on the Box.

I had many experiences on the box, but some I have already described in different chapters. So I would confine myself only to giving a few more, which I hope would be interesting to my readers.

In 1905 I was driving a horse with a vice of plunging forward, when once, while he was in the action of plunging, the rein gave way and I had no other alternative but to turn him round, which brought him to a standstill. Second time after a few months, while driving a team the off-rein gave way. In the same manner I got the leaders turned round to the opposite way and held the wheelers back.

In 1909 I had a pair of country-bred Tonga ponies to break in. The only vice in them was to jib within the Municipal limits of the town. To get rid of this vice I had to drive them separately with old horses in a light carriage for a few weeks which cured them all right.

It was once in the same year that I had a pair of a kicker and a plunger while driving in the city. I had to stop and then while I was starting, the plunger made a great plunge and put his fore-legs right across the pole, thus irritating the kicker to play his usual trick, and so I was rather in a difficult position to control them. The kicker did not remain contented with this, but tried further to bolt. No sooner he went kicking a few paces, I managed to collide with a lamp post which luckily saved a great accident. No damage was done either to carriage or harness except a few cut-offs to himself.